THE PROFESSIONAL YOU

Your Shortcut to Leverage Collective Wisdom From
Remarkable Achievers Around the World

Ginny,
Thank you for being
the professional you!

By Michael Giaimo

Contents

A powerful formula to create the best you,
based on a series of powerful quotes and
meaningful experiences

Dedication

I wrote this book to provide guidance for my two precious children, Tony and Alicia, with hopes that they share their experiences and accumulated knowledge with the world.

> *"You must be the change you wish to see in the world."*
> — Mahatma Gandhi

Tony and Alicia, you have been privileged with world experiences. These experiences include exposure to diverse cultures, international events, social and business realities, all of which mom and I had to manage effectively so that we may positively influence your development into adulthood. As a result, you should be able to fully appreciate, recognize and capitalize on my shared experiences and their subsequent learnings shared in this book.

> *"It is better to look ahead and prepare than to look back and regret."*
> — Jackie Joyner Kersee

Not to disappoint you, I included endless references to quotes throughout the book. I did this knowing that this is the only way you would expect me to share my knowledge. 😊

There is no doubt in my mind that you both will soon present a new and valuable perspective about being a "professional you" as you both have demonstrated throughout your childhood the ability to observe, learn and apply the many lessons and success traits that mom and I have shared with you.

"Make the world a better place one person at a time. Start with yourself."
—Linda Poindexter

Tony and Alicia, I am so very proud of your successes throughout your childhood and especially now as young adults. I wish you both continuous successes in adulthood. I love you!

Proud Dad

"The life you have left is a gift. Cherish it and enjoy it now to the fullest. Do what matters, now."
—Leo Babauta

Acknowledgments

To my enduring wife Misha. You changed my life! I never imagined the possibility that my vision of the "perfect" mate would, in fact, become my wife and the mother of my children. Not only did this become a reality, but also the pivotal moment in my young adulthood. As you know, I never contemplated marriage until I met you. The second I laid eyes on you I wanted to know you, and, as I did, it was clear that your belief in me, along with the way you challenged me, was the only way I could accomplish my vision of realizing "the American dream." So I chose you!

Your trust, admiration and encouragement gave me the most important tool I needed to succeed in anything I ventured in. From growing up as a responsible adult to growing as a professional, I give you 100% of the credit for the most critical ingredient which is self-confidence. The more than three decades I challenged myself to grow as an individual, and the many challenges I needed to overcome, would not have been possible without your great ability to level set with me, and of course, your moral and emotional support.

Thank you for believing in me, thank you for your endless patience, and **thank you** for the confidence that I so desperately needed. **I love you, my love!**

> *"It is our choices that show what we truly are, far more than our abilities."*
> —J.K. Rowling

Tony and Alicia, you gave me tremendous inspiration and a deep desire to become the best father, husband and professional. The standards you and I stand by (and the basis of being a successful professional) are the very things that brought me to write this book. This book is truly a product of the person you made me by being such precious children. **Thank you** for being R.I.C.H. 😊 in your lives.

> *"My wish for you is that this life becomes all that you want it to be. Your dreams stay big, and your worries stay small. You never need to carry more than you can hold and, while you're out there getting where you're getting to, I hope you know somebody loves you, and wants the same things too. This is my wish."*
> —Rascal Flatts

Mom and dad, I will always respect your life journey. The many experiences and challenges you had in your life which you shared with me became among the greatest lessons of life for me. More importantly, you have instilled in me the great gift of moral obligation, responsibility and hard work. I am very grateful for such gifts, which laid the foundation for my commitment as a father. I also thank you for giving me the privilege to visit and appreciate different cultures across the globe. This privilege allowed me to appreciate the diversity of many cultures, all of which broadened my perspective in life. **Mom and dad, thank you!**

> *"The only person who is educated is the one who has learned how to learn and change."*
> —Carl Rogers

To my siblings **Alain and Sylvie**. Our shared experiences and upbringing led to our common values, attributes, and work ethic. Although we truly have different characters as individuals, I am very confident our lifelong relationship and common experiences (as we grew up with great expectations and discipline) greatly influenced our characters and, essentially, became the foundation of our unique individuality. Mom and dad's "high standards" and tough discipline led to our strong values and individual attributes, which I am very grateful for. Alain and Sylvie, we may have different lifestyles and perhaps even different opinions about social and political issues, but what we have in common is resilience, hard work and the ability to never give up on our pursuit of excellence.

> *"When we seek to discover the best in others, we somehow bring out the best in ourselves"*
> —William Arthur Ward

I **thank you** for leading the charge and displaying the desired results our parents were hopeful for, and although it took me a little longer, your lifelong commitment to excellence convinced me that I too could essentially have the necessary discipline and pursuit of excellence. I **thank you** for your natural contribution to that foundation, and I am grateful that you both remain in my life. I forever love and respect you!

> *"Never forget where you've been. Never lose sight of where you're going. And never take for granted the people who travel the journey with you."*
> —Susan Gale

To my dear friends. I believe that many of the most valuable lessons in my life came from experiences you and I shared, as well as the many times you allowed me to lean on your shoulders and seek your wisdom to broaden my perspective. These experiences include personal experiences you had and, by sharing those difficult moments with me, you gave me numerous opportunities to reflect, learn and grow. I **thank you** for this precious gift.

> *"We all have the extraordinary coded within us, waiting to be released."*
> —Jean Houston

To my college professors, colleagues and professionals before me. Thank you for the continuous level set and for being exemplary during our day-to-day. The information, knowledge, successes and experiences you share with the world became my greatest resources in life. I continuously seek opportunities to learn from it all, and I hope others do as well.

> *"You must learn a new way to think before you can master a new way to be."*
> —Marianne Williamson

And to you (the reader) if you happen to be someone else other than Tony and Alicia, I commend you for your interest and recognition that we can all learn from just listening in. You are unique and you can learn from history. These two attributes create a gateway to discovering "The Professional You." One of the simplest ways to leverage your attributes and accelerate your journey is to capitalize on learning from reading and observing straight from the source. The most precious resources are people, and history identified influential people, many of whom left us with very impactful quotes.

These quotes are readily available; my suggestion is that you start there. For your convenience, I wrote this entire book based on quotes I read or heard throughout my lifetime. I believe these quotes shaped my character and, most importantly, continue to guide me through life with great success. You deserve to have this wonderful and rewarding experience, and you have a responsibility to pass it on to future generations. You have unlimited resources to learn, experience and share!

Introduction

We are not in a position in which we have nothing to work with. We already have capacities, talents, direction, missions or a calling."
—Abraham Maslow

Most of us consider ourselves "a good person," and most of us have a strong desire to succeed, at least in a professional sense. And some of us recognize the opportunity to continuously self-develop in a personal sense.

With seven billion plus people on earth, there is only one of you! You are unique and you can benefit the world with your unique attributes. Your skills and intellect may benefit a professional environment, or even society, or in your own family circle. However, too often we fall short of truly believing ourselves that we do have value. Is that also the case for you? Why is that? Is it because no one seems to notice or much less give us the opportunity to show your worth? Or is it possibly because you have yet to develop *The Professional YOU.*

"In the business world, everyone is paid in two coins: cash and experience. Take the experience first; the cash will come later."
—Harold Geneen

At one point or another in our lives, most of will have imagined that we won the lottery and won a million dollars! Yes, I know you would rather imagine that you won several millions so that you can go along with just about any scenarios I place in front of you.

For the sake of this exercise, I want us to stay with one million dollars; this way you can carefully consider the scenario and understand that the choices you make may outlive your winnings of a million dollars.

a. You have a million dollars readily available to you
b. None of your family members or friends know about your winnings
c. Your debts amount to <$100K (including vehicles and student loans)
d. Your mortgage balance is $200K
e. Your spouse is a homemaker, or you are simply not married
f. You have two small children (K-6)

If you are like most, you will have paid off your debt (minus the mortgage), bought yourself a toy or that one thing you always wanted, and considered the following:

a. Do I tell my family and/or friends?
b. Do I quit my job? (I've always imagined the ability to do so without thinking through it)
c. Do I start my dream business?
d. Do I give to my favorite charity?
e. Do I buy a new vehicle?
f. Do I move to my favorite city in the world?

If I missed something or perhaps suggested something that is out of character for you, don't worry about it. If we agree that you would most likely spend some of the money but not all, am I correct?

Now the question becomes what do you do with the remaining hundreds of thousands of dollars? More importantly, what are your thought processes and your outlook in life now? Isn't it funny how our perspective changes depending on our financial situation? Why is that?

If my assumption of your character as I described in the first paragraph is correct, the only thing that changed about you is your financial worth. You still mean well, you still have a strong desire to succeed, and you still present worth to society. Meanwhile, this proposed scenario of you winning the lottery might provide greater confidence in you that someone may, after all, recognize your worth and give you the opportunity you were looking for. So, what changed?

> *"I don't forgive people because I'm weak. I forgive them because I am strong enough to know people make mistakes."*
> —Marilyn Monroe

We live in a world where mainstream society views our worth based on our financial status. Our view of who we are, and our self-confidence, is greatly affected by the feedback we receive from our peers. In the age of "tic-toc," "fakebook" and "tweeter," users of these social media applications are continuously receiving messages to remind them of social trends which subsequently may remind us that we are not up to par! Social norms suggest that we are no more valuable than the people with similar financial statue than us. Do we need to change our financial status to change who we are? I trust you understand the message I am portraying here. Your self-reflection and attitude are the only characteristics about you that you need change, and the good news is that they are both free!

Let's go back to our scenario where you just won the lottery. What happens to your attitude, your confidence, and your sense of altruism? Are you as interested or bothered by the social messaging? Why or why not? There is no right answer here, just an opportunity for you to self-reflect. If you are truly a giving person, you will give no matter to your financial status. If you are truly a positive person, your attitude will reflect that. If you desire to give and desire to think positively, consider that you have endless opportunities to do so. Remember that old saying "If you think you can, you're right and if you think you can't, you're right." There is a little truth in that, isn't there?

> *"If you really want world-class success, decide today to stop caring what other people think and keep your own counsel. Others may or may not have your best interests at heart, but you always will. Calm down and listen to the little voice inside and have the guts to follow it. Trust yourself and know that if you're wrong you have the ability to bounce back. Caring about other people is an asset. Caring about what other people think is a liability."*
> —Steve Siebol

This is not a self-help book. You already possess and can naturally change any behaviors getting in the way of being the professional you.

The intent of this book is to convince you that you are already a professional in many aspects of your life, and success in your life is having the ability to identify and subsequently display these successful traits in all areas of your life. It begins with self-reflection and positive thinking. But, of course, this will require that you take on the challenge of managing social influence. You are unique and you have attributes that you and the world can benefit from. Do not allow social pressure to make you believe that you need to be someone else.

"Good people often make unethical decisions and don't even know it."
—Author unknown

The professionalism that you lack in your life is simply stored in your subconscious and, by considering the things I share in this book, you will be able to be conscious about your behavior and realize the "professional you" who you are meant to be!

"I keep my ideals, because in spite of everything I still believe that people are really good at heart."
—Anne Frank

Why should you be professional you?

*"The thing that is really hard, and really amazing,
is giving up on being perfect and beginning the
work of becoming yourself."*
—Anna Quindlen

This book is meant to be thought-provoking for you to consider the wisdom shared throughout history, and trigger a thought pattern that allows you to be more consciously competent to realize what

Throughout the next few chapters, I am going to share some of the personal learning experiences and consequential decisions I made in my ongoing journey to become the professional me; but, first, we need to talk about the elephant in the room. You are you and I am me so the professional you naturally are is not the professional me; hence what on earth am I hoping to accomplish here?

*"I know of no safe repository of the ultimate power
of society but the people. And if we think them not
enlightened enough, the remedy is not to take
power from them, but to inform them by
education"*
—Thomas Jefferson

Yes, you are you and I am me. Like in all industries and its businesses, most professionals bring unique skills and natural talents complemented by their unique characters. Life is no different than an industry and so we need "professional us" to emerge in greater numbers for the industry of life to flourish. "The professional you" is an asset to society and everyone (including me). We are not privileged with "your best" until you display "The Professional You!"

> *"Learning without thinking is labor lost; thinking without learning is dangerous."*
> —Chinese Proverb

Throughout our lives we received countless advice from relatives, friends, colleagues and even strangers. Interestingly, we tend to favor (or at least pay more attention to) strangers, and social media. Why is that? The truth is that the person with the greatest ability to influence you to change (should you desire it) is the person in the mirror. Yes, you!

Have you ever wondered why it is so difficult to influence or be influenced by the person closest to you (i.e. your spouse)? The truth is that the more time you spend with a person, the more likely you are to show your shortcomings and vulnerability; thus, creating an element of doubt and diminished credibility. Others (strangers) have not; yet wisdom can easily be gained from these engagements. But because strangers do not know who you truly are, it is easy for your subconscious to discard or downplay their advice; subsequently your self-esteem may lower and your attitude towards the desired change may not be as positive as it needs to be for you to action the change.

> *"There is a voice inside of you that whispers all day long 'I feel this is right for me, I know that this is wrong.' No teacher, preacher, parent, friend or wise man can decide what's right for you - just listen to the voice that speaks inside."*
> —Shel Silverstein

I was fortunate enough to grow up in a middle income household. As a family, we were not overly concerned about safety, nourishment or opportunities to be educated. Unfortunately, like many children no matter the financial status, for several reasons my childhood was challenging emotionally. I am not going to go into the details in this book because I want to keep the focus on the essence of the opportunity to be "The professional you" and not the reasons why you should. However, I am certain that many of you (readers) have similar stories from your childhood which may have created significant emotional trauma that you carried into your adulthood. The good news is that we have the immediate opportunity to overcome such emotional states and move forward with positive, enriching, and rewarding experiences. I discovered this possibility by leveraging the experience and insight of others around me. It should be no surprise to you that this book contains a significant number of quotes, all of which are meaningful enough to me that I live by them!

When my first born (Tony) presented me with the immediate challenge to demonstrate responsibility and integrity, as many parents do I felt the need to educate myself with several books on parenthood, fatherhood and behavioral science. I discovered effective techniques to parent and, most importantly, increasingly gained understanding of the importance towards transactional analysis (Eric Berne's findings around ego states). Engaging Tony in my proper ego states meant a greater ability to communicate. Subsequently, the continuous efforts (and shortfalls) towards improving my communication with Tony led to my own-self-discovery. A very humbling discovery which I believe has been the greatest contributor to the development of my character.

I trust you are reading between my words and extracting the key factors that will improve any of us as human beings. Let's put them together as I did with the help of my second born (Alicia). By the time Alicia entered kindergarten, it was clear to me that my children would benefit from consistent messaging. All of us are born as unique individuals and have different communication and learning preferences; nevertheless, we can all benefit from consistent messaging. As a result, I came up with an acronym that I believe depicts the ultimate success for a human being, and I inscribed it on the foot of each of my children's beds. The acronym is R.I.C.H. - Responsibility, Integrity, Character and Humility.

R.I.C.H.

I believe wisdom comes from our own personal experiences and learning from our failure, as well as other people's failures (seek opportunities to learn history and counsel from others). This book grants you an opportunity to leverage such wisdom. I am providing my own wisdom by sharing with you meaningful quotes and my personal experience actioning such statements. Quotes are indeed statements of reflection from various individuals who society deemed successful achievers (not necessary financially).

Your potential success of being the professional you is directly related to the wisdom you are willing to gain, and, most importantly, the behavior and attitude towards the foundation of your character which ensures your success to becoming the professional you. I call these fundamentals being **R.I.C.H.** (Responsibility, Integrity, Character and Humility). The remainder of this book supports my idea of being R.I.C.H. in my life.

R.I.C.H.

- Responsibility
- Integrity
- Character
- Humility

Responsibility

I find that the humbler we strive to become, the more responsible and accountable we tend to be. Responsibility is one of our character traits that we often pretend to flawlessly display; especially when observed by others. Meanwhile our observers view us in a different way. I see responsibility in the same light as ethics. We all would like to believe that we are ethical, and the truth is that we are, and we are not. You may consider yourself a good person, but you cannot deny that some of your decisions or behaviors are not as you would hope they would have been, and possibly infringing on your ethical standard. We are emotional beings. Our emotions often get in the way of our rational thinking; subsequently our behaviors may take a wrong turn….we are all biased and many times our decision-making is influenced by our bias.

Yale Psychologist, David Armor, suggests that we fall short of our self-perception and calls it an "illusion of objectivity." The good news is that we can protect our egoistic perception of ourselves and point out to other clinical findings which suggest that our bias is mostly unconscious bias; thus, not really consider a decision we make or an act we choose. Most importantly, although the bias may exist (unconsciously), many of us learn to manage it and overcome the temptation to reflect our subconscious natural being and, essentially, make the right decisions, and that is to act ethically of course. So, what's the point of all this? The point is that we either are, or eventually can be, professional ethical people. This learning behavior is a gift of society which becomes available throughout our life experiences; we call it "wisdom!"

> *"If you accept the expectations of others, especially negative ones, then you never will change the outcome."*
> —Michael Jordan

This quote renders many benefits to all of us. The person acting responsibly gains the personal satisfaction of "doing the right thing" thus eliminates the potential "guilt" or concern for not being responsible. Additionally, the responsible person most likely accumulates respect and trust. For the rest of us (recipients of the deeds from the responsible person), we are most likely freed from assuming that responsibility or from the need to challenge the person for not being responsible.

Responsibility also reduces the chances of something going wrong; hence enabling a better choice for everyone.

Sounds logical and easy to do right? So why do all of us fall short of being consistently responsible?

In my introduction to this book, I talked about ethics. If you remember, I suggested that our subconscious and bias challenges our desire to make good decisions.

> *"People can save the world by the way they think and by the way they behave and what they hold to be important."*
> —Cyndi Lauper

Let me suggest that the same is true when it comes to responsibility. No doubt in my mind that most of us strive to act responsibly, but often our judgment is clouded by ongoing physical or emotional realities (i.e., fatigue, anxiety, and depression etc.) which essentially compromise our ability to consider all the facts or comprehensively process the information we have received regarding the matter at hand. This results in poor judgment and the subsequent choice of not acting responsibly.

The only way I see us being more successful being responsible, is to constantly remind ourselves that we are a responsible person and must display our ability to always act responsibly. By testing my children on the meaning of R.I.C.H., I can reiterate the need of being responsible for them and myself alike.

> *"Don't get so anxious for something that you'll accept anything. Hold to your standards and be willing to walk away - heads up."*
> —Thema Bryant-Davis

Integrity

Not just a moral compass, but also a consistency in character.

"Right is right, even if everyone is against it; and wrong is wrong, even if everyone is for it."
—William Penn

A person with integrity is usually well regarded and more trusted. A label we should all strive to have. Mom may suggest I have this label, my wife may agree but others may have a different perception and it is imperative that our children, friends and co-workers view us as a person with integrity; thus, the need to be consistently aware of the perception we create. It is nearly impossible to influence people and gain favorable outcomes for everyone involved unless the perception of who you are is a positive one. "Perception becomes reality."

You most likely also have integrity, right? The problem seems to be with the people that don't know us or people that think they know us but clearly have a misconception of who we are. So, how do we fix that? We manage our action to create a positive perception of who we are, then we simply become!

"Think before you act," sounds familiar? I would even suggest thinking before you speak as well so that, if necessary, you may explain your thoughts and reasons behind your words or actions. At the end of the day, your words and actions are reflections of your character and integrity. Integrity should be your moral compass and consistency of character. Let me remind you of good advice you most likely received several times over the years, and that is "Don't say or do anything that we would not want our mother to hear or see." Be yourself and say what you mean and mean what you say.

> *"People are often unreasonable and self-centered. Forgive them anyway. If you are kind, people may accuse you of ulterior motives. Be kind anyway. If you are honest, people may cheat you. Be honest anyway. If you find happiness, people may be jealous. Be happy anyway. The good you do today may be forgotten tomorrow. Do well anyway. Give the world the best you have, and it may never be enough. Give your best anyway."*
> —Mother Teresa

Seek every opportunity to display integrity. If you do this in every aspect of your life (home, work, leisure activities etc.) you will essentially be recognized as a person of integrity by everyone that matters to you.

Simply because you earned it!

> *"In any moment of decision, the best thing you can do is the right thing. The worst thing you can do is nothing."*
> —Theodore Roosevelt

Character

Character is my absolute favorite word to reference. I think character reflects who we truly are, and it is defined by what we say and what we do.

Folks that know me know that I love analogies and I don't shy away from quotes either. To be consistent, I will do the same throughout this book. Here is my favorite quote on "character":

> *"Character is what you do when no one is looking."*
> —Author unknown

Pretty simple and straight forward. If you think about it, character is really a demonstration of any and all traits about yourself, so yes it includes the bad character traits. Knowing this, we should understand that if we master the easy "good" character traits then we quickly build a reputable and admirable character. Why not begin with ones like: oh, I don't know, responsibility and integrity?!

> *"To do great things is difficult; but to command great things is more difficult."*
> —Friedrich Nietzsche

Humility

You must admit that it is always pleasant and admirable to see someone humble. Yet, we often fall short of humility ourselves. Why is that?

Think back about the first paragraph I wrote in my introduction. Remember how I suggested that you are most likely a person of many qualities that is unfortunately not recognized as such. Is it possible that we take the opportunity to be bold about our successes because we are convinced that no one will know or recognize our successes if we don't mention them? We even do this with the obvious ones - you know what I mean – the successes that we have among our peers (and the successes that are noticed by family members). We may even exaggerate about some of our successes (especially if the audience did not witness the event). Why do we do that? Why is it that we find much more humility in older people than younger ones, especially among citizens of older cultures than ours, like those in Asia? Again, why is that?

> *"Begin challenging your own assumptions. Your assumptions are your windows on the world. Scrub them off every once in a while, or the light won't come in."*
> —Alan Alda

Much like wisdom, humility is developed with experience, hence from age. Yes, I know there are many youngsters out there that do demonstrate humility (my little girl included), but these individuals are exceptional and scarce. I would also suggest that, in many instances, the younger crowd that has this admirable character trait may have experienced something so significant (not necessarily dramatic) that every other experience and success in their life seems minuscule or not as significant in comparison. One tends to become humble as a result. Finally, the other aspect of humility which is often overlooked is the ability to laugh at oneself. Not a pleasant thing to do, but definitely a great way to demonstrate humility.

I am tremendously busy with work which provides opportunities and choices for my family. When I am not working, I write. Today, I am sitting in a charming local restaurant in the city of Quebec and I realize how blessed I am to be able to do what I am passionate about (developing people for their benefit and the benefit of our world); yet being compensated fairly, providing for my family and securing my retirement to enjoy with my bride who sacrifices as much as I do to secure our livelihood, and rarely receives the recognition for it; much less the compensation.

Attitude

There is no doubt in my mind that all of us can create a much better environment for ourselves if we live by, and live among, people who are R.I.C.H., but we cannot deny that, no matter our desire and no matter our circumstances, the biggest factor in our effectiveness to change our reality is to have the right attitude.

Attitude and behavior are shaped and influenced by the following:

1. Optimism

> *"I never saw a pessimistic general win a battle."*
> —E.E. Cummings

2. Accountability

> *"When a man points a finger at someone else, he should remember that four of his fingers are pointing at himself."*
> —Louis Nizer

3. Character

> *"The ultimate measure of man is not where he stands in moments of comfort and convenience, but where he stands at time of challenge and controversy."*
> —Dr. Martin Luther King

4. Learning

> *"Learning is the beginning of wealth. Learning is the beginning of health. Learning is the beginning*

of spirituality. Searching and learning is where the miracle process all begins."
—Jim Rohn

"Learn from yesterday, live for today, hope for tomorrow. The important thing is not to stop questioning."
—Albert Einstein

5. Communication

"Aerodynamically, the bumblebee shouldn't be able to fly, but it doesn't know it, so it goes on flying anyway."
—Mary Kay Ash

"You will never change your life until you change something you do daily. The secret of your success is found in your daily routine."
—John C. Maxwell

Develop a Plan

I know what you're thinking: "Here we go again, develop a plan, work the plan, set goals, and you will achieve your dreams...*cliché!*" *Right? Yes,* I admit it is cliché but just as many others; they exist simply because they are the common factor and recipe to success; yet, most people do not adopt this principle and choose to go about their lives by different means (mostly taking it a day at a time, overcoming obstacles as they come along with the subsequent heartaches and essential losses along the way).

So, why on earth do most people choose this route when in fact it most likely leads to falling short of one's goals? For this reason: I would suggest that the lack of creating a plan or setting goals is not a conscious decision, but rather sub-conscious. As a matter of fact, I believe most people believe that they do have a plan, and they do set goals, but they are simply not written down. Why does this matter? It matters because it is too easy to skip over a goal or fall short of a goal if it is not written down, and there are no accountability measures in place.

Imagine playing darts without a dart board! What are you aiming at, and what did you hit?

Hopefully I have said enough to convince you to write down specific goals to work a (written down) plan. Now, the question is how do I make a conscious decision to write down my goals? The answer is "attitude." Yes, another cliché, and yes, I am going to reference more quotes to support my case.

"Nothing can stop the man with the right mental attitude from achieving his goal; nothing on earth can help the man with the wrong mental attitude."
—Thomas Jefferson

The right **ATTITUDE** will give you the motivation and discipline you need to be **100%** on target.

One of my favorite discoveries is the **"substitution cipher"** where each letter of the alphabet represents a number *(a=1, b=2, c=3, d=4, e=5....... k=11... n=14... t=20... u=21... w=23... z=26).*

This discovery led me to a scholar's finding of an astonishing equation. The section below outlines the equation (alongside a series of quotes of course):

"Hard work beats talent when talent doesn't work hard."
—Tim Notke

HARD WORK = 98 (8+1+18+4+23+15+18+11)

"Genius is one percent inspiration, ninety-nine percent perspiration."
—Thomas Edison

In my opinion, the best way to get more is to give more; therefore, I strongly believe in capitalism and lean on the very well-known biblical command "You reap what you sow."

"Hard work spotlights the character of people: some turn up their sleeves, some turn up their noses, and some don't turn up at all."
—Sam Ewig

I recognize that hard work by itself does not guarantee success, but it certainly guarantees more than the alternative results from not working hard.

> *"Formula for success: Rise early, work hard, strike oil."*
> —J.P. Getty

Not working hard would be no different than not buying a ticket and expecting to win the lottery. You need to show up and take action to have a chance to receive the desired results.

> *"I find that the harder I work, the more luck I seem to have."*
> —Thomas Jefferson

The harder you work, the more opportunities you create for yourself. By simple definition, exposure gives greater visibility and opportunity to any potential contributors to your success.

KNOWLEDGE =
96 (11+14+15+23+12+5+4+7+5)

> *"The desire of knowledge, like the thirst for riches, increases ever with the acquisition of it."*
> —Laurence Sternne

The amount of knowledge you gain is a factor for the level of productivity you produce; there is a direct correlation to the results from your work efforts. I am sure you are familiar with the saying "work smart, not hard" so imagine if you did both (work hard and smart); naturally, the results will be much greater than with the singular input. Hard work + knowledge (multiplier) = greater results.

As much as knowledge seems to be key to greater success, the greatest contributor and factor is attitude! "Attitude is everything, right?" Yes, it is everything because the wrong attitude would naturally demotivate you from working hard and reduce the chances for you to be receptive to gain knowledge. Consequently, the result from your tamed productivity is likely to be unfavorable and certainly not from your best efforts.

ATTITUDE = 100 (1+20+20+9+20+21+4+5)

> *"The greatest discovery of all time is that a person can change his future by merely changing his attitude."*
> —Oprah Winfrey

Attitude is the one thing than we own "at will." Our attitude reflects in our actions which are most often re-actions to what we experience, see or hear. It is entirely up to us to decide how we are to react. The product of our reactions is the reflection of our attitude.

Optimism

A simple choice of believing that we can, rather than not believing. This principle is directly related to hope and considered to be enhanced by religious beliefs. No matter your faith, if you strongly believe, you will always be hopeful that any situation can be improved.

> *"Optimism is the faith that leads to achievement. Nothing can be done without hope and confidence."*
> —Helen Keller

> *"It's better to be an optimist who is sometimes wrong than a pessimist who is always right."*
> —Author unknown

> *"Every time you subtract negative from your life, you make room for more positive."*
> —Author unknown

Zig Ziglar is considered one of the most effective inspirational public speakers in our century. His messages are simple reflections of our own realities.

As an example, *Zig reminds us that "Positive thinking won't let you do anything, but it will let you do everything better than negative thinking will."*

> *"Once you replace negative thoughts with positive ones, you'll start having positive results."*
> —Willie Nelson

We live in a hypocritical world! We are fully aware of our shortcomings, especially if our shortfall was intentional, so I would argue that we lack accountability, and we are reluctant to hold someone accountable, since we do not want to talk about the elephant in the room that we constantly feed ourselves. The fact is that we can overcome this damaging behavior simply by holding ourselves and others accountable. Of course, it begins with self-accountability!

> *"The first to apologize is the bravest, the first to forgive is the strongest, and the first to forget is the happiest."*
> —Unknown author

"Think positive, be positive."

> *"The way to happiness: Keep your heart free from hate, your mind from worry. Live simply, expect little, except little, and give much. Scatter sunshine, forget yourself, and think of others."*
> —Norman Vincent Peale

> *"A man can be as great as he wants to be. If you believe in yourself and have the courage, the determination, the dedication, the competitive drive, and if you are willing to sacrifice the little things in life and pay the price for the things that are worthwhile, it can be done."*
> —Vince Lombardi

Experience

I strongly believe that the most valuable resource for any organization or family units are the individuals themselves. The very reason why I named my business Leverage Resources is simply because the most precious and valuable resource on earth is our human capital (You!), and not leveraging it is the greatest mistake any organization can make.

Our past and present experiences translate to great learnings, and if we choose to learn from these experiences and apply them to our day-to-day (personal or business) life, then we can improve over time. The benefit of learning from our own or other's experience, is the opportunity to improve our future.

> *"It takes a lot of words to say what you have in mind, give it more thought."*
> —Dennis Roch

The greatest gift we have in life is the ability to learn. No matter where we live or who we are, we can learn from anyone or anything around us. We can begin by learning from appreciation for the simple and complex nature surrounding us. We can learn by observing others, we can learn from history, and, more importantly, we can and should learn from our own experiences.

> *"Our learnings. Most people give up just when they're about to achieve success."*
> —Ross Perot

Learning

As I indicated in my acknowledgment, I am mostly grateful for the shared experiences and learnings from my family, friends and colleagues. The obvious benefit is that our shared experiences and learnings gave me the opportunity to improve my future.

> *"When planning for a year, plant corn. When planning for a decade, plant trees. When planning for life, train and educate people."*
> —Chinese proverb

The title of my book *"The Professional You"* is meant for you (the reader) to process the information I am sharing in relation to your own experiences so that you may reflect on your own learnings and commit to becoming the best "You." Professionalism suggests that you display excellence in a specific task, while maintaining full composure and respect to develop and maintain meaningful relationships. Full composure and respect can only happen if you are consciously competent about your behaviors.

Conscious Competence

The grandfather of psychoanalysis (Sigmund Freud) discovered that 6/7 of our reality is subconscious. When was the last time you thought about breathing? Yet, how many times did you breathe today? Most of our behaviors are based on habits driven by our subconscious, not decisions based on consciousness. They are emotional responses, not rational.

For you to be rational, you need to behave in your "adult" ego state, not your "parent or child" ego states.

As a child, you were mostly engaging a parent, teacher or other adults who would either nurture you or reject certain behaviors (no, don't, won't, can't etc.). The effect of a parent-child engagement is that one ego (parent) exercises power over the other (child). As a result, the child ego conforms or learns from the engagement. In contrast, the child quickly learns to leverage the desire from the parent's own nature; subsequently, the child appeals to the parent's emotions and possibly gets the parent to concede.

It is not until we separate our emotions and feelings from our behaviors that we can engage our "adult" ego state and engage our rational thinking. This is called conscious competence. To be clear, separating emotions does not mean becoming non-emotional as we are emotional beings after all! It simply means not allowing our emotions to control our behaviors. Rational thinking is to recognize our emotions and the natural subsequent behavior which is likely to create discomfort and trigger our "fight or flight"

without communicating (verbally or non-verbally) then engage a coping mechanism (whatever one you develop for yourself) that allows you to separate the emotion from your behavior whether it is addressing someone or deciding on a particular action.

> *"Act as if what you do makes a difference.*
> *It does."*
> —William James

Communication

Communication comes in many forms. Most of us acknowledge that we communicate with words or body language, but only a few people realize that our non-verbals, tone and speech fluctuation are the greatest contributors to our communication.

Albert Mehrabian determined that 55% of our feelings are communicated via non-verbals, 38% via tone and only 7% with words. "It's not what you say, but how you say it." Additionally, we fail to realize that some of our audiences have perceived notions of who we are even before we have the first opportunity to communicate with them. This dates to 9 BC where people routinely wore swords and daggers to the left side of their body messaging a potential intent to harm anyone in a proximity could be interpreted without a need to verbalize it. As a result, people felt the need to extend their right hand as they approach one another to notify the other party that they are not engaging with intent to harm. That non-verbal gesture is recognized today as the handshake gesture.

Effective communication can only be realized by adopting the following three principles:

1. Know your audience
2. Confirm receptivity and understanding
3. Gain favorable agreement

"Faced with the choice between changing one's mind and proving that there is no need to do so, almost everyone gets busy on the proof."
—Galbraith

Communication is key for every effort we make in our personal and professional lives, whether it is self-improvement, organizational development or relationship building. No one would argue that effective communication is a key element to influencing others, yet most people or organizations fall short with these elements. Why is that?

"If it takes a lot of words to say what you have in mind, give it more thought."
—Dennis Roch

"The true measure of a man is not the number of servants he has, but the number of men he serves."
—Arnold Glasgow

Our most important responsibility, which happens to have the greatest reward, is to develop and maintain meaningful relationships. Unfortunately, the level of success in developing relationships is directly related to our ability to effectively communicate and prioritize with minimum self-interest.

You cannot convince someone to see something that they do not want to see, no matter how much it would improve their lives.

"You have to love and accept them exactly as they are their own way, in their own time, if they ever choose to do so. Otherwise, you'll be giving them the power over your happiness, too."
—Doe Zantamata

Be Interested

A genuine commitment to improving communication is to be interested. A personal pet peeve for me is the unwillingness of the communicator to look in my eyes while addressing me. It distracts me from giving them my full attention. I understand and respect the fact that not all communicators have the comfort to look at you straight in the eyes while communicating with you. Not doing so diminishes the genuine intent to communicate. You can deliver a phrase while looking in the eyes of your audience and then look away to regain your comfort. You do not want to create the perception that the person is simply not interested in my emotions or ability to receive the message; they simply want to talk at you and not with you. By being interested, we also tend to be better listeners, and we can pay attention to whether the receiver gives us signs that he or she understood our communication. This is another important element of communication.

> *"Time is a companion that goes with us on a journey. It reminds us to cherish each moment, because it will never come again. What we leave behind is not as important as how we have lived."*
> —Jean Luc Picard

A Different World

Think about the most recent conversations you've engaged in. You began the conversation by greeting or acknowledging the person you engaged to gain their favorable attention (possibly a handshake?). The intent of your efforts was either to gain trust, or perhaps express a feeling that would foster trust. The question is whether you were successful or were you misunderstood. No matter the intent, because we have different perspectives and different interpretations about what we hear, we often fall short of successfully communicating. So how do we change this reality?

> *"Nature gave us one tongue and two ears so we could hear twice as much as we speak."*
> —Epictetus

Unfortunately, most of us did not have the opportunity to learn the fundamental skills to be an effective communicator until we became adults. So, unless you were privileged to learn the skills from your parents or educators from your early years in school, you are faced with the never-ending challenge of overcoming the inevitable potholes in the way of effective communication.

> *Be a good listener. Your ears will never get you in trouble."*
> —Frank Tyger

We mostly communicate with the same people day in, day out, and we can leverage what we know about the person, including the weight of their non-verbals, all of which is processed in our subconscious. So, if you need to communicate with someone you don't know, and you know there is a great possibility that you will not effectively communicate with them unless you understand their preferences in communication, why not do a little homework? Take a few minutes to learn about your audience prior to engaging. Use your resources (people and the internet) and do the homework!

I sincerely believe that most of us initiate our communication with positive intentions, and somewhere along the route we have a disconnect (most often not identified until the damage has been done). This creates a wedge in our efforts of effective communication. A clear disconnect is likely to be the misconception of what is communicated.

> *"Be strong enough to stand alone, be yourself*
> *enough to stand apart, but be wise enough to stand*
> *together when the time comes."*
> —Mark Amend

Misinterpretation is due to our failure to understand our audience and, consequently, failure to manage our tone, posture or vocabulary during the delivery of our message. From a speaker's perspective, the route of misconception in communication is the simple fact that the listener only heard the words spoken but did not really listen to the message. Sometimes it is not intentional, it is simply us not being consciously present because our subconscious has pre-occupied us with other pressing matters.

"When I do good, I feel good. When I do bad, I feel bad. That's my religion."
—Abraham Lincoln

I came to America as a young man who did not speak a word of English. As a result, I never really learned proper English. I learned American! Over the years, I learned that I mispronounced so many words that they meant something other than what I intended to communicate. I have learned that many words have multiple meanings, especially if when challenged. If you look up the "English definition" of many of the words we use in our daily vocabulary, you will come to the same realization I have, which is the strange reality of the vocabulary used by most Americans does not really support what is being communicated, and simply does not make much sense!

You know how frustrating it is not to be understood or to be put under scrutiny because someone misinterpreted what you said and translated your message into a misconception. It is at times embarrassing, and at times an opportunity for your family, friends or colleagues to tease you. I know my kids enjoy always teasing me about mispronouncing words. Nevertheless, we need to own the miscommunication and fix it. Otherwise, we run the risk of being misinterpreted and the implications may be great. I have learned this lesson in my marriage when both parties are limited in vocabulary or the pronunciation thereof. My wife and I do not have a common first language, and we run into occasional disconnects simply due to our limited ability to effectively communicate in English. You may benefit from asking a follow-up question that can only be answered as a reiteration of your message. It is imperative that you manage your messaging and acknowledgment of receipt of your message. This creates accountability that your audience successfully received your message.

If not received, then you simply failed in your communication, and you should re-visit my three suggested principles of communication (know your audience, check for understanding and gain favorable agreement).

> *"I can't change the direction of the wind, but I can adjust my sails to always reach my destination."*
> —Jimmy Dean

The cold war officially ended when the Berlin wall was taken down in November of 1989. This created an opportunity for two different worlds (West and East, Communists and Capitalists) to directly influence their respective cultures. A new reality that was considered an impossible dream for so long and that neither region began to appreciate until the 1990s. Even today (3 ½ decades later) we have major differences in our cultures which include fundamental beliefs, preferences and behavior habits that challenge our intellect based on our respective world views.

Behaviors begin to mimic other people's behavior around them; thus, the foundational saying **"You become who you hang around."**

Like most parents, I press my children to live by my values and principles (being R.I.C.H.). I do this because I believe that my values and principles are the most respectful and most valuable to society. I am willing to bet that your parents or you (if you are a parent) are no different.

> *"You were born to win, but to be a winner, you must plan to win, prepare to win, and expect to win."*
> —Zig Ziglar

For this reason, I chose to consistently remind my children of my expectations for behaviors they would display. I chose to reference quotes to support my efforts, and I noticed my son's interest and appreciation for quotes and acronyms, hence **R.I.C.H**.

Childhood

Most of us benefited from learnings from our parents or other adults watching over us while offering their wisdom. Trust and respect were instantly present in our relationship with these adults, but most likely diminished during the transition to adulthood - a natural cause with some positive outcomes (i.e., self-confidence and a greater desire to achieve more etc.), and simultaneously a drawback to wisdom. This led to gaining experience with unfortunate unnecessary challenges as adolescents. We could have easily avoided these if we maintained trust in and respect with these adults. Possibly the very first thing many of us would have done differently is to listen and apply the many suggestions! 😊

> *"If your parents ever measured you as a child, they had you stand against a wall, and made a little pencil mark on the wall to show your growth, they did not measure you against your brother, or the neighbor's kids, or kids on TV. When you measure your growth, make sure to only measure your today self, by your past self. If you compare your relationships, your success, or your anything against anyone else, you are not being fair to you. Everyone has a different path, a different pace, and different challenges to face along the way."*
> —Doe Zantamata

Wisdom - How do you know?

Just because you were told a thousand times and just because you learned it from your parents, and from media sources, internet and/or in school, it does not make it so.

"Many receive advice, only the wise profit from it."
—Harper Lee

"Victory always starts in the head. It's a state of mind. It then spreads with such radiance and such affirmations that destiny can do nothing but obey."
—Douchan Gersi

History is created by people who believed or did something other than what they were told or learned. Can anyone or anything be greater than what is known unless someone believes that it can? Without belief, it is unlikely that it will ever be.

"You have only one life, and no one else will live it for you. Shouldn't you take the time right now to figure out what that life is all about?"
—Harry Browne

Everything we have learned and admired from history was essentially the "future" in someone's mind. It took a person's imagination, dream and inspiration, accompanied by a commitment to let their dream become a reality, before it became history to future generations. Most of us did not truly reflect on our experiences as a child until adulthood. Ironically, our reflection (as adults) is often in conjunction with our observation of a specific behavior the new generation displays. The challenge is that we observe from our perspective based on our own experiences and not the perspective of the individual(s) being observed. It is a challenge because it is not relatable, and it is difficult to influence in the same light as it was for our caregivers advising us from their perspective.

"Remember the two benefits of failure. First, if you do fail, you learn what doesn't work; and second, the failures give you the opportunity to try a new approach."
—Roger Von Oech

No matter what country you grew up in, I think you would agree that your generation in comparison to subsequent generations, had to work harder to accomplish just about anything. This is a simple fact based on the evolution of our society, whereas technology continues to develop, social equality progresses, and products and services are expected to be more readily available and of higher quality. As a result, today's society can produce more results in less time and with less effort.

This new reality brings us back to the reflection of our childhood where one can appreciate the simplicity of our lives gradually disappearing in the event of the evolution of our social expectations and abilities. Our sub-conscious allows us to act without much thought or contemplating of our behavior. These experiences collectively created "filters" which determine the way we act or react to things we see or hear. Most of us create similar filters as others within our social environment. This is due to our having similar experiences, hence a common culture.

One common contributor to most cultural upbringing is media. Media comes in many forms including books, films, documentaries, and news, etc. Most of which are now typically accessed via the World Wide Web (aka the WWW or the internet). We can argue that our future is a product, or at the very least shaped by media, especially films and novels.

Every child, and hence many adults, are inspired and motivated by what they read or watch. As a result, their creative minds work with what they absorb in these films and novels and create our future!

"Great things are not accomplished by those who yield to trends, fads, and popular opinion."
—Jack Kerouac

Cultures are cherished by individuals in like cultures, but not necessarily appreciated or respected by others in different cultural environments. This is due to the difficulties in our ability to relate or adapt to such different cultures, ultimately leading us to judging and even prejudice. This phenomenon is the source of disagreements in relationships (personal and professional) and severe tension including those directly related to politics and world affairs.

"Immature people always want to win an argument, even at the cost of a relationship. Mature people understand that it's always better to lose an argument and win a relationship."
—Author unknown

Our cultural awareness becomes a factor in our success. Our ability to adapt and thrive in various cultures is a great asset and can be a clear advantage associated with our cultural diversity. Whenever we take the initiative to learn about other cultures (foreign and local) or can experience various cultures, we are improving our ability to communicate and persuade others by being more relatable and less confrontational.

In retrospect, as a "dreamer" I created opportunities to achieve unbelievable things and, most importantly, become who I am (oops, I failed to display humility). Back to my point, I strongly believe that we need to be dreamers, create a clear vision of who we can be and what we can do, and develop behavior that displays great passion, commitment and discipline to achieve desired results (our dream).

> *"Don't count every day of the week; make every day of the week count."*
> —Mark Amend

Dream big, develop a plan that nurtures your dream, and discipline yourself to create a consistent behavior that allows you to work the plan.

"Don't let anyone or anything keep you from achieving your dream." A cliché perhaps, but I assure you it is also a reality that we must face every day. Our closest loved ones, our respected teachers and mentors, and our trusted resources, they all essentially create barriers to our chances of success. Yes, many support our efforts and even our dreams, and for that reason they are necessary influencers, but also keep in mind that unless they achieved the very thing you are trying to achieve, they are naturally a barrier by being an example and a constant reminder of the possibility that you will not become....

> *"You must either modify your dreams or magnify your skills."*
> —Jim Rohn

I implore you to always display all your unique values and attributes and allow the observer to witness "The Professional You."

> *"The great thing in this world is not so much where we stand as in what direction we are moving. To reach the port of Heaven, we must sail sometimes with the wind and sometimes against it - but we must sail, and not drift, nor lie at anchor."*
> —Oliver Wendell Holmes, Sr.

You must think and act differently and abide in your dream with the endless possibilities of you realizing the dream. Once you are locked into your dream, you are ready to develop and execute a plan. Of course, it begins with setting goals (specific action steps and a timeline to work the plan, with accountability measures). Once you achieve your goals you should challenge yourself with a new set of goals and continuously improve (black-belt improvement cycle).

> *"The only man who makes no mistakes is the man who never does anything. Do not be afraid to make mistakes providing you do not make the same one twice."*
> —Theodore Roosevelt

> *"You will never do anything in this world without courage. It is the greatest quality of the mind to honor."*
> —James Allen

"The easiest thing to be in the world is you. The most difficult thing to be is what other people want you to be."
—Leo Buscaglia

We need to be dreamers to be great achievers. Understandingly, dreamers are more scrutinized than "non-dreamers," and yes also more likely to fail or suffer more setbacks than "non-dreamers." In retrospect, dreamers create opportunities to become and to achieve:

- Dreams create vision
- Vision develops passion
- Passion nurtures commitment and discipline
- Commitment and discipline create results
- Results create **history**

Think back about the first time you reflected on the purpose of life. Did you conclude that *your* purpose of life is simply to be? Or did you come to conclusion that any one's purpose of life is to achieve? Yes, I understand that what you seek to achieve is very likely different from what I or anyone else hopes to achieve, or maybe you are not even sure about what it is that you are looking to achieve, but nonetheless you are looking to achieve! So you agree that your and my purpose is to achieve, hence the dream. The question becomes whether our dream is alive or not.

"People are attracted to you by what they see in you; they remain attracted to you by what you see in yourself."
—Mark Amend

The Philosopher

You are no more and no less of a philosopher than Mr. Plato, Aristotle, or John Locke, all of which are listed among the greatest in history.

> *"Life will give you whatever experience is most*
> *helpful for the evolution of your consciousness.*
> *How do you know this is the experience you need?*
> *Because this is the experience you are having at this*
> *moment."*
> —Eckhart Tolle

Think about it. Each of us is unique. We are born as originals and throughout our lives we encounter different people and have different experiences; subsequently, we begin to resemble one another, and perhaps even become a copy of those surrounding us. We are unique individuals, with different perspectives, perhaps even different philosophies on life; yet we spend a lifetime trying to become a person we admire. Why is that? Is it possible that we are conditioned and influenced to become that person (alternate to who we truly are)?

> *"The state of your life is nothing more than a*
> *reflection of your state of mind."*
> —Dr. Wayne W. Dyer

Your unique values, attributes, skills and yes wisdom are as valuable to society as those of Aristotle, Plato or anyone equally admired may have offered to the world.

> *"Life is an opportunity, benefit from it. Life is*
> *beauty, admire it. Life is a dream, realize it. Life is*

a challenge, meet it. Life is a duty, complete it. Life is a game, play it. Life is a promise, fulfill it. Life is sorrow, overcome it. Life is a song, sing it. Life is a struggle, accept it. Life is a tragedy, confront it. Life is an adventure, dare it. Life is luck, make it. Life is life, fight for it."
—Mother Teresa

If you have not done so already, I implore you to go to the nearest park or outdoor café (preferably on a busy day) and observe the "wisdom" that everyone around you displays. This includes children, as well as animals! Why? Because the wisdom that children and animals display is most likely not yet saturated with the opinions of adults or people in general. That wisdom is purely from instinct. Yes, we all have it but too often forgot it or chose not to employ it because of "peer pressure" or what is deemed "socially acceptable."

"One of the deep secrets of life is that all that is really worth doing is what we do for others."
—Lewis Carol

Procrastination

"If you spend too much time thinking about a thing, you'll never get it done."
—Bruce Lee

Why do we procrastinate to begin with? We do this for one of two reasons: we either know that someone (possibly ourselves) will end up on doing what it is that we postponed for the moment, or it is not important to us, and we simply do not care if it does not get done. In either case, the act of procrastinating is very damaging to our character, and it affects others around us, which are implications that must be considered. Based on my position regarding our conscious and sub-conscience, I argue that procrastination feeds the monster, including the lack of confidence that we can achieve desired results and our observers who believe we are not as reliable as we suggested we were. Even if you dread to do something that may not be rewarding or that requires flat out pushing of yourself, delaying its course only prolongs the agony and anticipation of the inevitable painful moment.

How often do you put off until tomorrow what you could easily accomplish today?

I propose you don't procrastinate and get it over with! You may also find out that not procrastinating has rewards on its own. You may determine that it was not as bad as you thought or, better yet, was rewarding after all. Also, don't forget that removing the opportunity for someone to think less of you may be rewarding in itself.

"Tomorrow is often the busiest day of the week."
—Spanish proverb

*"Time is an equal opportunity employer. Each
human being has exactly the same number of hours
and minutes every day. Rich people can't buy more
hours. Scientists can't invent new minutes. And
you can't save time to spend it on another day.
Even so, time is amazingly fair and forgiving. No
matter how much time you've wasted in the past,
you still have an entire tomorrow."*
—Denis Waitley

Incompetence!!!

"It is not enough to stare up the steps, we must step up the stairs."
—Vaclav Havel

In the last paragraph, I talked about a sore subject (procrastination). This paragraph I would like to talk about one of the biggest culprits leading to "incompetence".

"In a hierarchy, every employee tends to rise to his level of incompetence."
—Laurence Peter

Unfortunately, I must admit that I accuse quite a few people of being incompetent, or as Webster defines it "lack ability". I don't know if I am not being fair in my assessment, or if I need to look more in the mirror and realize that maybe we are all deemed incompetent at times, so please help me decide because I wish for you to appreciate and leverage the values people offer and not experience the same frustration that I have on this subject. Besides, there are too many people out there who care about competence, and they use due diligence and work hard to get it right so they deserve the opportunities that seem to be in the hands of incompetent people.

"The noblest search is the search for excellence."
—Lyndon Johnson

Success is simple. Do what's right, the right way, all the time."
—Arnold Glasow

Consider the following examples of behavior and decide if these represent incompetence or are simply facts of life:

1.   **You call customer service (any company) to make a proactive change so that there is no error or confusion with whatever matter is at hand.**

   a.   Days or weeks later, you realize that you wasted your time because customer service did not make the change or communicate the change to the responsible department. As a result, your service or billing is now compromised.

   b.   Maybe I just have bad luck, but this situation seems to happen too often, and I am convinced that most customer service teams out there are full of incompetent people and just a waste of time.

2.   **Your co-worker (could even be your boss or direct report) failed to read the email that gave him/her specific instructions for what needed to be done.**

   a.   This same co-worker now sends you an email inquiring on the subject because it is "the first they heard of it."

   b.   Of course, you are now making an additional attempt to inform them.

   c.   Potentially, you are now having urgency on your hands because what did not get done now needs to be done "yesterday!"

3.   **Your co-worker (yes, I know I had another urgent matter come up...) decided to take a short cut and not due diligence with this. As a result, the organization or customer is now in need of immediate correction.**

a. Your resources are now compromised to respond to this emergency, and you are now forced to postpone other projects, your department loses credibility, the customer loses faith in your organization and your family now must wait additional time before you can make yourself available to them.

The good news for those of us who live in a capitalist country is that competition created by our "free market" allows us to choose who we do business with, so we do not need to continue engaging the same "incompetent" people if we choose not to. Oh wait, I realize there are exceptions.

> *"To solve any problem, here are three questions to ask yourself: First, what could I do? Second, what could I read? And third, whom could I ask?"*
> —Jim Rohn

> *"The world has the habit of making room for the man whose words and actions show that he knows where he is going."*
> —Napoleon Hill

The Strategist

My original thought of strategy was derivative of a plan to quickly achieve results by developing a competitive differentiator. I viewed strategy as a roadmap to effectively execute that plan so you can argue that my strategy was my approach of doing anything I set out to do. I later determined that my thought process was, in fact, causing me not to have a strategy at all! The plan itself should include milestones and specific goals which, in essence, is the roadmap, thus not the strategy. The only aspect of my thought that was on point is the notion that the strategy leads to a competitive differentiator. The strategy is, in fact, the unique differentiation you bring to the approach of the plan; hence, strategic in the sense that it defies the norm and considers what others did not.

Everyone has a perspective, and although some people may have a similar perspective, they certainly have different thought processes mainly due to their individual experiences; hence, filters as we discussed in earlier chapters.

As mentioned in my earlier chapters, you are born an original so no sense suggesting that you are no more than a duplicate of a colleague or mentor. You have your own attributes and aspirations, thus, should have your own strategy. This strategy may end up being the differentiator or unique approach that allowed you, your department or organization to effectively achieve the plan.

This new perspective on strategy should bring us full circle back to the opening of this paragraph where strategy is imperative for you to fulfill a purpose given your unique approach and roadmap. For this reason, more and more organizations develop strategies at department levels and even consider engaging a "subject matter expert," aka strategists, who naturally have not been affected by the organization's culture.

Define Success

Are you among the popular who define success by the level of recognition and accumulated wealth? Sure, you can argue that these are achievements, and they should be recognized as success, but in what sense and in whose eyes? And does success lead to happiness?

> *"Life's challenges are not supposed to paralyze you, they're supposed to help you discover who you are."*
> —Bernice Reagon

I strongly believe that the quest to pursue success and even the word itself, are both detrimental to the person wearing the label, and it does not necessarily lead to happiness. Most people I know (met or heard about) who are deemed successful are no happier than many who do not wear the label. The label is assigned and articulated by observers who measure success by the two means mentioned in my opening paragraph, and not by the person who is deemed successful. In fact, I know many of us (deemed successful) who would argue that their success is not defined in the same manner as being recognized or wealthy, but rather by their own belief of whether they have accomplished meaningful purpose in life and feel content that the remainder of their journey is a continuation of their accomplishments.

> *"What you get by reaching your destination isn't nearly as important as what you become by reaching your goals - what you will become is the winner you were born to be!"*
> —Zig Ziglar

I think of success as the ultimate peace of mind one can have no matter how busy, challenged, or chaotic events may be around them. I sincerely believe that if you feel you made a meaningful difference in people's lives and left a legacy or even modest memory that you made a difference, then you were undoubtedly successful! This form of success cannot be judged, criticized, labeled or even taken away as it is everlasting and so personal to you and the people positively affected by it.

> *"The primary cause of success in life is the ability to set and achieve goals. That's why the people who do not have goals are doomed forever to work for those who do. You either work to achieve your own goals, or you work to achieve someone else's goals."*
> —Brian Tracy

My mom said it best. Not sure how old I was, nor do I remember whether she quoted from someone or not, but I do remember that it made such a difference that I often (every time I am challenged by a critic) remind myself of these words. As mom says:

> *"The true treasures are accumulated in Heaven, not on earth."*
> —Mom

Goal Setting

Yes, I am going there again and this time deeper into the subject. I want to make sure that I leave you with a roadmap so that you have absolutely no excuse not to goal set, and, most importantly, achieve your goals!

> *"I consider a goal as a journey rather than a destination. And each year I set a new goal."*
> —Curtis Carlson

> *"When a goal matters enough to a person, that person will find a way to accomplish what at first seemed impossible."*
> —Nido Qubein

> *"If you have a goal, write it down. If you do not write it down, you do not have a goal - you have a wish."*
> —Steve Maraboli

Most of us know this is an imperative element of success, but we fail to do it. At least we don't do it properly, we don't write down our goals, we don't set timelines, we don't write down action steps directly related to our goals. Why is that? Well, if you are like me, you feel you are the exception and your goals are so clear in your mind that you are convinced that they are part of your continuous thought process (sub-conscious); therefore, everything we do is directly related to our goals and do not need to be written down! But if not written down, then it is unlikely you will achieve your goals, at least not anytime soon.

"If, in 10 years, you were to look back at your actions of today, what would you change? Always be asking yourself in terms of your goals and how you want to live."
—Craig Ballantyne

To put things in perspective, let's use this book for example. I set a goal to write this book in 2005 (a product of my inspiration and increased confidence as I saw my children grow to be amazing human beings). This book was not finished until December of 2015 and first published in 2016. What is more is that it was published without being edited and the editing stage was not complete until this year (2021)!

The amount of work I put into it certainly did not take me 10 years; clearly nothing more than procrastination! Not writing down my goal along with action steps and specific timelines is the very reason why this book was not written in 2005. Imagine if in May 2005 I wrote down the goal to complete my book by December 2006? My specific action steps would be to write no less than one page per day no matter what challenges each day brought to my schedule (or mood). This would result in me writing an excess of 500 pages by the due date of December 2006. You could argue that many of the pages would have not been written in the best circumstances and perhaps would consist of irrelevant thoughts, but I am very confident that out of the 500 pages I could salvage enough material to complete my book in a matter of days. Get my point? 😊

> *"There is no one GIANT step that does it, it's a lot of little steps."*
> —Peter Cohen

> *"It is a mistake to look too far ahead. Only one link of the chain of destiny can be handled at a time."*
> —Winston Churchill

Hopefully this proves my point that unless we write down the goal, without "mapping out" the objectives desired to be met, we have no direction and we are unlikely to arrive to our destination in a timely manner, or not at all! Why take a chance not to arrive, and why create the unnecessary delay with the inevitable challenges when all we need is to create a visual plan to see our turn-by turn, step-by-step direction, and then get on the road. This is an investment of just a few minutes to conceptualize, a few seconds to write down, and one minute to revisit on a daily basis so that we remain confident that we are traveling in the right direction, we are increasingly closer to our goal, and will, without a doubt, arrive to our desired destination.

> *"The best way to get started is to get started. Life rewards action... not reaction. Wait for nothing. Attack life."*
> —Dave Kekich

> *"The major reason for setting a goal is for what it makes of you to accomplish it. What it makes of you will always be the far greater value than what you get."*
> —Jim Rohn

"If you don't design our own life plan, chances are you'll fall into someone else's plan. And guess what they have planned for you? Not much."
—Jim Rohn

"What makes any person a leader is his or her ability to set goals and achieve desired results - nothing more, nothing less."
—Linda L. Martin, Dr., David G. Mutchler, "Fail-Safe Leadership."

SMART goals should be written down in the following manner:

Specific - (Can't hit a bull's eye if you throw darts at a dartboard that is missing the bull's eye, can you?) A specific written goal is clearly understood by anyone reading it no matter their familiarity of the author.

Measurable - The only way to know if you hit your goal is to measure the results against the starting point. (How close did you get to the number you aimed at on the dart board?)

Attainable - You can't throw darts at a board you don't own, so make sure your goals are attainable given what you have.

Realistic - You can't hit a bull's eye with a hand throw of a dart from 1,000 feet away, so make sure your goal is in relation to your reality.

Time specific - If you don't have a timeline, your goal becomes one of millions that will never be accomplished given the argument that the timeline has not come yet (much like most of your New Year resolutions! 😊)

> *"Dream big, but allow yourself the opportunity to start small, and have your share of struggles in the beginning. The world's greatest composers weren't writing symphonies the day they first sat at a piano."*
> —Kevin O'Rourke

"I will lose weight this year" is not specific or measurable or time bound. "I will lose 50lbs by January 15" may not be attainable or realistic if I am 180lbs and it is December 31st.

"I will lose 5lbs by January 15, 2022" is SMART!

Please accept a challenge to write down a goal that can be met in a matter of days, one that you failed to accomplish over the years so that it has meaning to you. Be sure to make it a SMART goal and **do not** shortcut the process (including daily affirmations towards your goal).

> *"If you can't fly, then run. If you can't run, then walk. If you can't walk, then crawl, but whatever you do, you have to keep moving forward."*
> —Dr. Martin Luther King, Jr.

> *"The greatest results in life are usually attained by simple means and the exercise of ordinary qualities. These may, for the most part, be summed in these two: common sense and perseverance."*
> —Owen Feltham

Perseverance

Staying true to our convictions and refusing to quit is the only way to ensure success. Think about the number of success stories which include accounts of overcoming obstacles or sustaining losses. None of them would be success stories if it was not for "perseverance." This attribute is critical and a "must have" for the professional you.

> *"Great works are performed, not by strength, but by perseverance."*
> —Samuel Johnson

Obstacles and unfortunate events are inevitable for all of us. This is often labeled with "accidents happen." So, to simplify the need for us to persevere knowing that these accidents will happen, I suggest we consider wearing seat belts!

You hate it, but you love the idea that it can save your life. Kind of like teenagers not liking parental guidance but loving the idea that parents are responsible for their safety and welfare.

If you were unfortunate enough to experience a car accident, but you were witted enough to have been buckled in prior to taking the road, you were probably extremely grateful that the seat belt worked exactly as you were told it would. How different is that from a teenager that was told "no" to a shady gathering, later to find out that the kids that did go ended up in trouble by being in the wrong place at the wrong time (and most likely with the wrong people). Maybe not the best compared analogy, but I think you get my drift. Kids: listen to your parents when they privilege you with their wisdom because it will most likely save you from something you do not want to experience.

"No life ever grows great until it is focused, dedicated, disciplined."
—Harry Emerson Fosdick

"Conscious repetition of positive affirmations will, in time, lead to your subconscious mind also producing positive and empowering thoughts. These positive thoughts will lead to positive beliefs about yourself and your life. These positive beliefs will lead to positive habits. And positive habits will lead you to a life of happiness and success."
—Author unknown

Affirmations and Bullying

Most of us heard of affirmations and most of us understand the effects of bullying, but how many of us believe in the impact of affirmations to the point of adopting the practice of making these affirmations on a regular basis? How many of us believe in the effect of bullying to the point we give careful consideration of our actions and words **prior** to acting or speaking?

> *"Words have special powers. The power to create smiles or frowns. The power to generate laughs or tears. The power to lift up or put down. The power to motivate or de-motivate. The power to teach good or evil. The power to express love or hate. The power to give or take. The power to heal or harm. Choose your words carefully."*
> —A.D. Williams

Neuroscientists have collected and analyzed data and confirmed impact and positive change to human behavior for subjects who routinely speak positive affirmations. This behavioral change is directly related to the conditioning (aka programming) of the subconscious, whereas the individual routinely seeks positive outcomes no matter the situation. The behavior also leads to greater engagement in a mental and physical capacity; whereas the individual becomes more engaged and productive in their day-to-day, often increasing their ability to achieve desired results, hence a likeliness for repeat in setting goals and creating new affirmations.

> *"A goal without a plan is just a wish."*
> —Larry Elde

Most recently, social media has increasingly recognized the presence of bullying and its negative impact; especially for the "tween" generation. Yet, the most recognized vehicle for this disgraceful act of bullying is in fact social media. The unfortunate reality is that most of us are simultaneously victims and guilty of bullying. The reason is that most individuals who bully, are doing so in retribution or due to conditioning from their immediate circle of influence where they themselves are being bullied on a regular basis. My attempt here is not to create an excuse for the act, but rather to give you an opportunity to reflect, recognize, and act by giving additional thought to your actions and words, especially when responding to what you deem to be an attack of some sort.

> *"Action is a great restorer and builder of confidence. Inaction is not only the result, but the cause, of fear. Perhaps the action you take will be successful; perhaps different action or adjustments will have to follow. But any action is better than no action at all."*
> —Norman Vincent Peale

The power of repetition. If you are old enough to read this book, you are old enough to know that enough repetition will essentially become a natural state in your life. Most everything we have learned was a series of repeated information (words, images, exercises, and routines etc.), whether it was in school or from continuous marketing exposure (commercials) or repeated behavior. The magic formula seems to be 12 weeks of repetition (or a thousand times). You will likely progress towards your goals, if not achieve them! Likewise, I challenge you to consider the effect of your actions or words. Let it be positive at every turn!

> *"If you believe that you can - you are right or if you believe that you can't - you are right."*
> —Author unknown

The ability to control thoughts and self-talk is critical to your own personal and professional success.

> *"Of all the people on the planet, you talk to yourself more than anyone. Make sure you are saying the right things."*
> —Martin Rooney

Mother Teresa spent most of her adult life (45+yrs) caring for the poor and the sickest people in the streets of Calcutta. She did this despite numerous warnings from the church that she may lose her sisterhood and, ultimately, the protection of the church. As a matter of fact, she provided care in the midst of her own poverty and insisted on not receiving recognition or praise for her service. The selfless life she lived was a testimony to her humility and faithfulness to her God. She claimed that her mission was one of love, not duty.

> *"God loves a joyful giver... A joyful heart is a normal result of a heart burning with love. Joy is strength."*

> *"Destiny is not a matter of chance; it's a matter of choice. It is not a thing to be waited for; it is a thing to be achieved."*
> —William Jennings Bryan

You are born an original and your perspective on every aspect of life is no more right or wrong than anyone else's. I am a firm believer that all three egos I referenced earlier are imperative to our development and can benefit us greatly when managed properly.

Experts like Eric Berne took a deep dive into Freud's philosophy around egos and "your three selves."

We essentially become adults and when we do, most of the time we try to act like one. Unfortunately, our "child" and "parent" get in the way, and we end up with foolish or excessive authoritative behavior. As a result, our conscious mind is conflicted and our behavior becomes too difficult to manage. The interesting thing is that it is often our natural behaviors that are deemed inappropriate and that often trigger our "adult" ego. As a result, we elect to behave as an adult even if it means being hypocritical based on our true beliefs. We need to be accepted by society and any other behavior would not be acceptable. When we properly manage our three selves, this allows us to be more social, respectful, wise, patient and compassionate. I call this wisdom!

> *"Learn the art of patience. Apply discipline to your thoughts when they become anxious over the outcome of a goal. Impatience breeds anxiety, fear, discouragement and failure. Patience creates confidence, decisiveness, and a rational outlook, which eventually leads to success."*
> —Brian Adams

Final Thoughts

This is the conclusion to my attempt to "meducate" you and convince you that you are indeed unique and valuable to society. Well done in completing your goal to read this book. By doing so, you demonstrated discipline, respect, humility, and the desire to do it right (I call it integrity). If there is any value in the beliefs I expressed throughout the book, you just added that value to your character!

My stated beliefs, life learnings and thought process are a product of my experiences reiterated by endless quotes which I noted mostly over the last 20 years. If this book did not offer valuable thoughts for you to contemplate and hopefully act upon, I suggest you revisit the series of quotes throughout the book and ask yourself, have any of these people (quoted) realized success or admiration whereas their words should at least be considered? Notwithstanding these quotes may be different in words, but similar enough in context, which is most likely not a coincidence and perhaps their message being the very thing their owners have in common. For this reason, I chose to end this book with a series of additional quotes with the hope that some will resonate... and lead you to "The Professional You."

"Just because you've made mistakes doesn't mean your mistakes get to make you. Take notice of your inner critic, forgive yourself, and move on."
—Robert Tew

"You are good enough, smart enough, beautiful enough, and strong enough. Believe it and stop letting insecurity run your life."
—Thema Davis

"If you look to others for fulfillment, you will never truly be fulfilled. If your happiness depends on money, you will never be happy with yourself. Be content with what you have; rejoice in the way things are. When you realize there is nothing lacking, the whole world belongs to you."
—Lao Tzu

"Treat others as if they were what they ought to be and help them become what they are capable of being."
—Unknown

"Nobody can go back and start a new beginning, but anyone can start today and make a new ending."
—Maria Robinson

"Everybody in your situation has the same choice: you can rue your situation, or you can dedicate yourself to changing it. Accept responsibility for the future. Refuse to complain, criticize, or condemn."
—Mark Ford

"Out of intense complexities, intense simplicities emerge."
—Winston Churchill

"Success is walking from failure to failure with no loss of enthusiasm."
—Winston Churchill

"If you have a strong commitment to your goals and dreams, and you wake up every day with a passion to do your job, everything is possible."
—Chantal Petitclerc

"Nothing is impossible;
the word itself says 'I'm possible'!"
—Audrey Hepburn

"Even if you fall on your face, you're still moving forward."
—Victor Kiam

Success is the ability to go from failure to failure without losing your enthusiasm."
—Winston Churchill

"Opportunity does not knock, it presents itself when you beat down the door."
—Kyle Chandler

"You can have anything you want if you want it badly enough. You can be anything you want to be, do anything you set out to accomplish if you hold to that desire with singleness of purpose."
—Abraham Lincoln

"Obstacles are those frightful things you see when you take your eyes off your goal."
—Henry Ford

"Life is like a bicycle. To keep your balance, you must keep moving."
—Albert Einstein

"A man is not finished when he is defeated. He is finished when he quits."
—Richard M. Nixon

"Develop success from failures. Discouragement and failure are two of the surest steppingstones to success."
—Dale Carnegie

"Each problem has hidden in it an opportunity so powerful that it literally dwarfs the problem. The greatest success stories were created by people who recognized a problem and turned it into an opportunity."
—Joseph Sugarman

"Success is not measured by what you accomplish, but by the opposition you have encountered, and the courage with which you have maintained the struggle against overwhelming odds."
—Orison Swett Marden

"For true success, ask yourself these four questions: Why? Why not? Why not me? Why not now?"
—James Allen

"Think of yourself as on the threshold of unparalleled success. A whole clear, glorious life lies before you. Achieve! Achieve!"
—Andrew Carnegie

"Every human has four endowments - self-awareness, conscience, an independent will, and creative imagination. These give us the ultimate human freedom... the power to choose, to respond, and to change."
—Stephen Covey

"Time decides who you meet in life, your heart decides who you want in your life, and your behavior decides who stays in your life."
—Author unknown

"There are three secrets to managing. The first secret is to have patience, the second is to be patient, and the third most important secret is patience."
—Chuck Tanner

"Believe in yourself, never give up and go about your business with passion drive and enthusiasm."
—Peter Jones

"When you reach for the stars, you may not quite get one, but you won't come up with a handful of mud either."
—Leo Burnett

"You can never have an impact on society if you have not changed yourself."
—Nelson Mandela

"You can never quit. Winners never quit, and quitters never win."
—Ted Turner

"Do something today that your future self will thank you for."
—Author unknown

"Choose a job you love, and you will never have to work a day in your life."
– Confucius

"The difference between what you were yesterday and what you will be tomorrow is what you do today."
—Stephen Pierce

"The gratification comes in the doing, not in the results."
—James Dean

"Never, never, never, never give up."
—Winston Churchill

Index

The bulk of my writing is based on my reflection from my life experiences to date; however, it is worth noting that my reflection has been, and continues to be, influenced by my reading. I strongly believe that continuous and systematic (at every opportunity) reading goes hand-in-hand with personal growth. As a result, it is imperative that each of us develop and maintain discipline and read no less than a dozen books (educational) a year; accompanied by daily readings of current events (worldwide), new developments (technology and science), and inspirational thoughts (quotes or historical events).

Please consider including the titles noted below to your list of books to read. They are the books that I drew knowledge from while writing this book. Perhaps you can set a goal to read each of these books over the next 24 months☺!

1. The Upside of Stress by Kelly McGonigal, PhD
2. The Purpose-Driven Life by Rick Warren
3. The Optimization Edge by Stephen Sashihara
4. Jonathan Livingston Seagull by Richard Bach
5. Strong Fathers, Strong Daughters by Meg Meeker
6. The Moral Sense by James Q Wilson
7. Quiet Strength by Tony Dungy
8. George C. Marshall by Forrest Pogue
9. How to Become an Overachiever by David E Carter
10. The World is Flat by Thomas L Friedman
11. Your Best Life Now by Joel Osteen
12. A People's History of the United States by Howard Zinn
13. Created to Win by Kevin Baerg

14. Something to Smile About by Zig Ziglar
15. Father to Son (or Father to Daughter) by Harry Harrison Jr.
16. America: Imagine a World Without Her by Dinesh D'Souza
17. All I Really Need to Know I learned in Kindergarten by Robert Fulghum
18. Strategic Management by Arthur Thompson
19. Communication For Managers by Norman Sigband
20. Coach Yourself to Success by Joe Moglia
21. Don't Sweat the Small Stuff by Richard and Christine Carlson
22. Fahrenheit 451 by Ray Bradbury
23. Value Merchants by Anderson James C.
24. The Art of Exceptional Living by Jim Rohn

Made in the USA
Columbia, SC
25 January 2022

54164652R00048